GW01110653

Original title:

We Promised Each Other No Gifts, But I Couldn't Help Myself

Copyright © 2024 Book Fairy Publishing

All rights reserved.

Editor: Theodor Taimla

Author: Marlen Vesiroos

ISBN HARDBACK: 978-9916-763-10-0

ISBN PAPERBACK: 978-9916-763-11-7

Touched by Undisclosed Love

In shadows cast by moon's soft glow,
A love concealed begins to flow,
Whispers only silence knows,
In hidden hearts where feelings grow.

Eyes that meet but dare not seek,
A thousand words they could not speak,
Bound by secrets, strong yet meek,
In quiet corners, spirits peak.

Through veils of dark, their passion gleamed,
A silent pact in starlight dreamed,
Two souls entwined, or so it seemed,
In unlit realms where hopes are deemed.

A touch, a glance, so fleeting real,
Within, a storm they could not seal,
A symphony they softly feel,
An undisclosed love they can't reveal.

Their hearts in quiet wonder thrived,
In moments stolen, dreams arrived,
Though paths diverge, they feel alive,
In shadows where their love survived.

Beyond the Unseen Barriers

Beyond the walls that time has grown,
Lies the truth we have not known,
Invisible but not alone,
In realms where seeds of hope are sown.

Barriers that hearts transcend,
Where spirits break and then they bend,
In whispers, messages they send,
Love's journey finds its rightful end.

Through trials that seem to ever last,
Encounters with the painful past,
A bridge of dreams we choose to cast,
Together, moving forward fast.

Hands that reach beyond the night,
Hearts that feel through all the plight,
In unity, we see the light,
Barriers unseen, take flight.

In the spaces where fear hides,
In the void where sorrow abides,
Together as one, we defy the tides,
Love and hope, our guiding guides.

Beneath the Surface of Promises

Whispers soft in twilight's cloak,
Dreams we weave in words half-spoke,
Beneath our vows lies something true,
A hidden pledge in world askew.

Stars that glimmer, bold ignite,
Lighting paths through endless night,
Promises like secret streams,
Ripple through the wondrous beams.

In hearts shadowed, hope resides,
Surfaced trust where love abides,
Glimpses bright of what could be,
Woven tight in you and me.

Loving Beneath the Vow

In the silence of heartbeats, profound,
Love whispers without a sound,
Beneath each vow, a story told,
In chambers of the heart, so bold.

Touch of hands, a bond unseen,
In quiet moments lies serene,
Promises that hold us tight,
Through darkest hours and endless night.

Gaze of love, a silent vow,
Eternity hidden in the now,
Upon this path, we gentle tread,
Together 'til the world is shed.

The Unseen Ribbon

Invisible threads that bind,
Love's ribbon, pure and kind,
Woven through our every thought,
In bonds unseen, but dearly sought.

Brush of hands, a fleeting sign,
Twined in whispers, soft, benign,
Paths converge and hearts align,
In love's embrace, a grand design.

Though the ribbon may not show,
Its presence, deep we ever know,
Entwined in hearts, a silent plea,
Together, through eternity.

Secret Offerings

In twilight’s hush, secrets kept,
Love's true offerings adept,
Whispers carried on the breeze,
Promises in quiet ease.

Soft caress of moonlight’s gleam,
Where soul to soul begins to dream,
Hidden gifts in shadows cast,
Love’s embrace forever lasts.

Through the veil of night, they dance,
Hearts entwined in tender trance,
Secret offerings, love’s pure art,
Shared between two kindred hearts.

The Gift Beyond Words

A whispering breeze of evening's grace,
Unfurls petals, delicate lace.
Stars adorn the silent night,
In whispers, darkness takes flight.

Eyes that speak of ancient lore,
A bridge of souls, forevermore.
Glimpses caught in shadowed dance,
Hearts entangled, by mere chance.

Voices lost in tangled dreams,
Truth unraveling at the seams.
Silent echoes, secrets heard,
The gift beyond our mortal word.

Unexpected Ties of Love

In every fleeting glance we bear,
Unseen threads weave through the air.
In chance encounters, moments spun,
Frayed edges of a world undone.

A spark ignites in twilight's glow,
Love blooms where least we know.
In shadows cast by moonlit skies,
Hearts find their bond, no goodbyes.

A touch, a smile, a gentle sigh,
Binds more tight than meets the eye.
In serendipity's embrace,
Unexpected ties leave trace.

Breaking the Silence with Joy

In the quiet whispers of dawn,
Rays of hope turn shadows gone.
Laughter breaks the silent curse,
With every note, the heart is nurse.

From the stillness, melodies rise,
In joy's refrain, our spirits ties.
Each echo soft, each sound so pure,
In laughter's arms, we find our cure.

The silence bows to voices bright,
Illuminated by love's light.
In every joyful, ringing laugh,
We find the path, our souls unmask.

Love’s Unplanned Gifts

In corners where the shadows play,
Love finds a gentle, hidden way.
Unscripted moments, pure and free,
In silent vows, just you and me.

The world may turn in haste and blur,
But in our hearts, a timeless stir.
Unexpected, undenied,
In love's embrace, nowhere to hide.

Life’s canvas painted unaware,
With gifts that show how much we care.
In every glance, each tender kiss,
We find in love, unplanned bliss.

Beneath the Promise

In twilight's tender embrace,
Dreams weave through silent skies.
Soft whispers paint the horizon,
As stars in slumber rise.

Hopes are anchored deep within,
Where shadows dare not roam.
Love's light guides the weary heart,
To find a fleeting home.

Promises beneath the stars,
Are bound by velvet night.
Echoes of forgotten vows,
Take flight to find their light.

In the quiet of the dawn,
Where day and night conspire,
Tomorrow's breath ignites the flame,
Beyond the world's desire.

Silent Celebrations

Within the silence of the eve,
Joyful whispers softly creep.
A dance of hearts in quiet realms,
Where memories safely sleep.

Candles flicker, shadows play,
In rooms of muted cheer.
Moments held in still embrace,
Their essence drawing near.

Laughter echoes in the mind,
Though lips may never part.
The spirit's song, a silent hymn,
Beats softly at the heart.

Each breath a pause in melody,
A note of hushed delight.
In these quiet celebrations,
We find our hidden light.

Unplanned Affection

In corners unexpected,
Love blooms in secret shades.
A glance, a touch, too fleeting,
In twilight it pervades.

No script to guide the passion,
No lines for each embrace.
It’s here in whispered moments,
We find our sacred space.

Eyes that speak in volumes,
Words caught on the air.
Unplanned and pure affection,
Unshackled, free from care.

In the serendipitous meeting,
Of hearts that beat as one.
No plans, just pure connection,
Beneath the endless sun.

Wrapped Sentiments

In letters bound with ribbon,
In tokens held with care.
Sentiments are woven tight,
In hearts that memories share.

Each word a stroke of kindness,
Each gift a silent vow.
Emotions wrapped in paper fine,
Unfold the here and now.

In the folds of careful thought,
Love’s essence finds its place.
No sound, yet deeply spoken,
In gesture and in grace.

Though time may fade the ribbons,
And tokens lose their sheen.
The sentiments we've wrapped with love,
Remain in sight unseen.

Transgressions of the Heart

In twilight’s gentle, somber hue,
A heart's transgressions come to view.
Forbidden love, a secret song,
Dances where it doesn’t belong.

Whispers linger in the night,
A silent plea for absent light.
Choices made beneath the stars,
Shadowed wounds, eternal scars.

Passions roar like tempest seas,
Silent prayers on bended knees.
What’s denied by daylight's grace,
In shadows finds a sacred place.

Memories stitched with threads of gold,
Stories of the heart, untold.
Transgressions, though they may depart,
Leave a map upon the heart.

Treasures Beyond Promise

Beyond the edge of twilight’s gleam,
Lie treasures found in boundless dream.
Promises of what could be,
Locked within the heart's decree.

Yet treasures hold a secret key,
A whisper of eternity.
Glimmers of a life once spun,
Where stars and hearts align as one.

Promises, though softly spoken,
In time are either kept or broken.
Treasure what the soul can find,
In moments free, unconfined.

So chase the whispers through the night,
Find treasures in the fading light.
For promises are fragile things,
Bound by what tomorrow brings.

Whispers of Forbidden Joy

In shadows cast by moon's soft glow,
Whispers of forbidden joy do flow.
Stolen moments, time's deceit,
Hearts in secret places meet.

Echoes of a love denied,
In the silence, side by side.
Joy, though cloaked in dark attire,
Kindles hearts with secret fire.

Eyes that speak where lips dare not,
Feelings that the world forgot.
Whispers held by stars above,
Forbidden joy, illicit love.

In twilight's veil, hearts conspire,
Drawn together by desire.
Forbidden though the paths they tread,
In whispers, endless dreams are fed.

Silent Agreements Broken

In the quiet, deals were made,
Promises that softly fade.
Silent agreements shaped our world,
In whispers, dreams and thoughts unfurled.

Yet trust, a fragile, fleeting thing,
A bird with broken, shattered wing.
Silent promises once spoken,
Leave hearts wounded, faithless, broken.

Eyes that met in silent trust,
Now look away in tearful dust.
Agreements shattered by a glance,
Lost in life’s uncertain dance.

In the aftermath of words unspoken,
Lie the remnants, worn and broken.
Silent, now the heart does weep,
For agreements it could not keep.

Heartfelt Exceptions

Within the bounds of day and night,
Exceptions shape our tender plight,
Moments rare, a soft delight,
Reveal the love, in ardent light.

When skies grow dark, and hearts feel sore,
These deviations soothe and roar,
A beacon bright, a gentle core,
In quiet acts, we feel much more.

In shadows long, and whispers small,
The heart discerns each secret call,
An unexpected, sweet enthrall,
In loving arms, we gently fall.

A world of rules, yet still we see,
Exceptions break monotony,
In you, I've found what love can be,
A timeless, pure infinity.

Whispering Surprises

Beneath the moon's soft, silver veil,
Lies whispers, where the stars regale,
Surprises spring without a tale,
Life's hidden truths, in hearts prevail.

In quiet corners, silence speaks,
Of moments bright, though often meek,
True love appears in gentle peaks,
Whispering secrets, all unique.

With each dawn, a blend of hues,
Presents a gift, a subtle muse,
An unseen hand begins to choose,
Great wonders, from the simplest cues.

In every breeze, a story's told,
Surprises made from feelings bold,
Life's meaning, hidden in the fold,
Of whispered dreams, forever gold.

Unseen Devotion

In shadows cast by light of day,
Unseen devotion finds its way,
Silent acts, with love to stay,
Woven deep in lives at play.

A glance, a touch, a gentle smile,
Unheard vows that bridge each mile,
Soft gestures pure, devoid of guile,
Reflect a love, both sweet and vile.

Though often missed by hurried eye,
These moments sacred, never die,
In heart's own memory, they lie,
Proof of care in how and why.

The world may not, this bond, behold,
Yet every act, a story told,
Unseen devotion, fierce and bold,
In hidden love, our souls enfold.

Subtle Offerings

In quiet dawn, when dreams are soft,
Subtle offerings aloft,
Of love and care, so often lost,
In moments small, true hearts exhaust.

A whispered word, a gentle hand,
Unseen, but deeply understand,
These offerings, like grains of sand,
Create a life, both vast and grand.

Not always loud, nor always seen,
True love resides in what has been,
In how we act in space between,
Life's fleeting, transient, routine.

From silhouettes, of twilight's gleam,
Subtle offerings softly stream,
They weave a love, beyond a dream,
Creating bonds, that fate redeems.

Beyond the Echo of Promises

Whispered dreams in twilight gleam,
Hopes that linger, softly beam.
Stars above that silent sway,
Guide us on our hidden way.

Promises like shadows cast,
In the heart, forever last.
Love that dances in the air,
Binding souls beyond compare.

Echoes of a future bright,
Shine within the darkest night.
We strive onward, undeterred,
By the whisperings we've heard.

Treasure the vows, gentle and pure,
In this world, they make us sure.
Far beyond the echo's call,
Lies a truth that conquers all.

The Silent Gift

In quiet moments, hearts do find,
A gift bestowed, so pure, so kind.
Whispers of the soul's sweet song,
In the silence, we belong.

Unspoken words that touch the heart,
From this world, we feel apart.
Yet in silence, voices blend,
Forming secrets without end.

Through the hush of morning light,
Love emerges, burning bright.
Not in sound, but in a gaze,
Passion found in silent praise.

A gift unseen, yet deeply felt,
In our silence, hearts have knelt.
For in the still, where none drift,
Lies the beauty of this gift.

The Secret of Kindness

A gentle touch, a silent deed,
Plants the most enduring seed.
Acts unseen, but brightly shine,
Through the veil of time, divine.

Kindness whispered, never loud,
Forms a silver lining's shroud.
In each heart, its roots entwine,
Love and warmth, a secret sign.

From a smile, a world can grow,
Into havens none would know.
Far beyond the common strife,
Simple kindness changes life.

In the shadows of our day,
Secret kindness lights the way.
Gifts unbidden, hearts set free,
From a seed, a thriving tree.

Transcending Silent Agreements

In silent pacts, we find our peace,
Agreements that will never cease.
Eyes that speak where words would fail,
Heartfelt vows that will prevail.

Beyond the spoken, shadows blend,
Understanding without end.
Hand in hand, in silent grace,
Journey shared, no empty space.

Through the muted depths, we soar,
Bound by truths we can't ignore.
In the hush, a world is spun,
Two as one, a love begun.

Silent vows, a bond refined,
Transcending words, purely aligned.
In this quiet, we transcend,
Silent agreements, without end.

Hidden Delights

In shadows cast by evening’s glow,
Where whispering winds in secret blow,
There lie delights unseen by day,
Where moonbeams dance and shadows play.

A world unfolds within the night,
With stars that twinkle, faint but bright,
In corners where the day is blind,
Such hidden gems you’ll often find.

Beneath the surface, calm and still,
Lies beauty waiting, thrice the thrill,
For those who dare, who seek, who yearn,
To hidden paths, their hearts return.

In whispered tales and muted light,
Unseen until the fall of night,
These pleasures, dear, for those who seek,
Hidden delights, elusive, meek.

The Unplanned Surprise

In the shadows of routine, it lies,
A wonder, pure, an unplanned prize,
A spark ignites when least we seek,
A joy profound, a peak in pique.

An unexpected twist in time,
A melody without a rhyme,
When life's script swerves from path once set,
A fresh surprise, not known as yet.

In moments marked by sweet delight,
New chapters written pure and bright,
No plan foretold, no course designed,
Yet in those turns, our hearts aligned.

So cherish well those breaks in stride,
Where unknown joys in shadows hide,
Amidst the routine, look and see,
The unplanned brings true harmony.

Beneath the Ribbon’s Secret

A ribbon wrapped in hues so deep,
Conceals a secret, tight to keep,
Beneath its folds, a wonder there,
A hidden gift with love and care.

Unwrap the layers, soft and slow,
For what's beneath you'll come to know,
A token pure, a heart’s delight,
Inself contained, yet out in light.

Within the folds of tender weave,
A tale unfolds, you won’t believe,
For underneath the ribbon tight,
Lies all that's true, and pure, and right.

Gaze into the secret held,
Where ribbon’s end and truth have meld,
With open hearts, we find the gleam,
Beneath the ribbon’s secret dream.

Unexpected Tokens

In quiet moments, tokens found,
Appear without a sight or sound,
Unlooked-for gifts by fate bestowed,
On paths uncharted by our road.

These tokens come in varied means,
As whispered words in twilight scenes,
In acts of kindness, pure and bright,
Unseen by day, revealed by night.

Their value lies not in their weight,
But in the love they cultivate,
For tokens small can hold the key,
To hearts unlocked, and spirits free.

So cherish these, the gifts untold,
In unexpected forms they mold,
A tapestry of love and grace,
In each token’s warm embrace.

Love’s Silent Renegade

In shadows where soft whispers fade,
Silent renegades of the heart,
Their passion’s unyielding parade,
Love’s silent renegade, pure art.

Through corridors of secret dreams,
Hushed footsteps softly intertwine,
In twilight’s silver-tinted beams,
Two souls in clandestine design.

No words are spoken, none are missed,
Eyes converse in furtive glint,
Each touch a silent, tender tryst,
Love’s quiet rebels leave their hint.

As moonlight bathes the night in peace,
Their fervor seeks no grand acclaim,
In quietude, their joys increase,
Love’s silent renegade, untamed.

Heartfelt Contraband

In the stillness of the night,
Contraband of the heart does flow,
Whispers soft in candlelight,
Secret love only we know.

Forbidden glances steal the air,
Heartfelt treasures, hidden deep,
A clandestine tender care,
Promises our souls do keep.

Through veiled dreams and unseen ways,
Passion's trade defies the rule,
Each heartbeat a rebel's phrase,
Love's outlaw, fierce and cool.

Stolen moments, valued more,
In the quiet, our hearts stand,
While the world's judgments ignore,
We hold tight, our contraband.

Whispered Exchanges of Kindness

In the hush of morning’s light,
Whispers weave through peaceful air,
Kindness blooms with tender might,
Secret gifts, hearts laid bare.

Silent words through gestures speak,
Gentle hands caress the soul,
Each soft touch, affection’s peak,
Whispers make the broken whole.

Eyes that meet with silent grace,
In their depths, compassion’s sea,
Kindness wraps in soft embrace,
Love’s exchange, so tenderly.

Through the quiet, bonds are formed,
Hearts entwined in subtle blend,
Acts of kindness, unadorned,
Silent love that knows no end.

Unexpected Tokens of Affection

In moments when least expected,
Tokens rare do make their way,
Love's tender gestures, undetected,
Soft surprise brightens the day.

A smile in passing, light and warm,
Words that heal and gently mend,
Small acts defying the norm,
Tokens of a love, unbend.

Through the everyday's routine,
Unexpected gifts appear,
Touch of grace in mundane scene,
Affection's path, sweet and clear.

When the world feels cold and gray,
Subtle gestures turn the tide,
Tokens given in quiet sway,
Affection's essence, glorified.

Lovingly Unwrapped

In the silence, gifts we find,
Bonded hearts, forever kind.
Moments cherished, wrapped in light,
Love’s embrace, both pure and bright.

Words unspoken, eyes that gleam,
Shared together, life’s sweet dream.
Understanding, deep and clear,
In your presence, no more fear.

Gentle touch, so tender, sweet,
With you, my world is all complete.
Laughter echoes, joy profound,
Happiness is all around.

Promises in every tear,
Strengthened vows with every year.
In your warmth, my soul’s confined,
Joy in you, my perfect find.

Fleeting Persuasions

Morning whispers, fleeting grace,
Hopes and dreams in quick embrace.
Moments shifting, swift and bright,
Dawn’s illusions, out of sight.

Wind’s persuasion, soft yet strong,
Guides the heart where it belongs.
Transient joys, like morning dew,
Vanish in a breath anew.

Chasing echoes, shadows play,
Promises that fade away.
Living in the now, unchained,
In each second, life retained.

Fleeting moments, memories fade,
In their wake, new paths are laid.
Life’s a dance, so ever brief,
Embrace now, beyond belief.

Heart's Uncontrollable Urges

Uncharted paths, the heart does pave,
To love's call, the soul is slave.
Passions wild, untamed and free,
Yearning, longing, destiny.

Whispers soft, a sweet allure,
Love's addiction, the only cure.
Boundless dreams, emotions surge,
Heart responds with unconrolled urge.

Eyes that tell what lips cannot,
Signaled love in every thought.
Compelled by forces, deep and true,
Heart's desires, always new.

Fire that consumes, burns so bright,
Guided by the heart's own light.
To follow urges, one must dare,
Love's journey, beyond compare.

Beyond Promises

In the whispers of the night,
Futures cast in softened light.
Promises are just the start,
What we hold is in our heart.

Words once spoken, fade away,
But in actions, they will stay.
Beyond the vows, a bond so deep,
Trust in love, forever keep.

Stars that witness, silent skies,
Telling tales where truth lies.
Not just words but deeds that show,
Love's true depth, a steady glow.

Beyond the promises is real,
Every moment, hearts reveal.
With each breath, our love renews,
In your eyes, my every truth.

Surpassing Our Boundaries

Beyond the lines we dare to trace,
We venture to a boundless place.
With every step, a whispered dream,
Together we become a team.

No walls confine our vivid quest,
We seek the stars, we chase the best.
In unity, we scale the dawn,
With every challenge bravely gone.

The world expands as fears dissolve,
Through courage found, our hearts evolve.
Hand in hand, through night and day,
Exploring paths in a grand array.

With vision clear, we forge ahead,
On trails where few have lightly tread.
In strength, in hope, our spirits fly,
Surpassing limits set so high.

In Defiance of Agreement

Voices rise in fierce defiance,
Breaking silent, silent alliance.
Out of shadows, truth takes flight,
In boldness, we reclaim our right.

Where nods and sighs have held us fast,
New discourses, they burst at last.
We challenge norms, disrupt the calm,
In defiance, we find our psalm.

Conformity once draped like chains,
Now shattered by our fierce refrains.
In every word, a fire burns,
In every heart, a voice returns.

We break the ties so tightly bound,
In dissonance, our power found.
Together, yet unique, we stand,
In defiance, we take command.

Unintended Acts of Devotion

Quiet gestures, unseen love,
Whispers sent to skies above.
In shadows, kindness finds its way,
Unintended, though it may.

Every moment, grace revealed,
With hidden warmth, our spirits healed.
In silent acts, devotion grows,
Through gentle winds, affection blows.

No grand display, no show of might,
In tender deeds, a pure delight.
Unspoken care, a light unseen,
In subtle ways, a soulful sheen.

In every touch, a story told,
Of love that blooms in depths untold.
Without intent, pure hearts align,
In acts of care, our fates entwine.

Rules Meant for Breaking

In every word, a boundary laid,
In every rule, a choice delayed.
Yet in our hearts, a fierce refrain,
Some paths are meant to break the chain.

For every 'no,' a daring try,
For every fence, a chance to fly.
In every challenge, we find grace,
In every barrier, an open space.

With bold resolve, we bend the norm,
Defying storms, we find our form.
In every break, a spirit freed,
In every crack, the light we need.

The lines we've crossed, the risks we face,
In bold revolt, we find our place.
In breaking rules, we forge anew,
With every step, the world we drew.

The Heart's Silent Offering

In whispers soft, I lay my plea,
Beneath the stars, where dreams run free.
A token birthed from tender thought,
A silent gift, with love enwrought.

The nightingales in shadows sing,
Their melodies on moonlit wing.
Within the night, my heart implores,
To be the one your soul adores.

Through silent sighs and quiet prayer,
My passions swirl within the air.
The whispered winds, they carry forth,
A promise of unmeasured worth.

Beneath the crescent's gentle glow,
My feelings stream, an endless flow.
Without a word, the heart does speak,
A love profound, though silent, meek.

The Unseen Act of Love

In every glance, a word unsaid,
An act of love, in silence bred.
No grand display, no voice to shout,
Yet meaning deep, it echoes out.

Hands that brush, a tender feel,
In gestures small, our hearts reveal.
The quiet deed, the unseen care,
In hushed embrace, emotions bear.

A look, a smile, a fleeting touch,
It speaks of love, it says so much.
No need for words, no need for sound,
In stillness, whispers can be found.

Love's language soft, beyond the voice,
In silent deeds, we find our choice.
So let our actions gently show,
The silent love we both bestow.

Against the Silent Pact

Against the night, where shadows play,
A silent pact my heart defrays.
It battles not with words or might,
But steers by love, against the night.

In moon's embrace, the silence falls,
And softly echoes through the halls.
Against the pact of quiet night,
My soul seeks dawn, a brighter light.

The stars, they wink with eyes so bright,
As if to see my heart's true plight.
Against this vow of silent seas,
I wish to speak of love's decrees.

In stillness deep, the silence reigns,
Yet love, unbound, breaks all its chains.
Against the night's unspoken lore,
My heart will cry for evermore.

Hidden Sentiments Revealed

In shadows deep, where secrets lay,
Hidden thoughts come out to play.
Underneath the quiet veil,
Our hearts' true whispers, we unveil.

The hidden smiles in fleeting glance,
Revealed in moments of romance.
Unbidden words from souls concealed,
At last, the truth of love revealed.

In silent rooms, emotions rise,
Beneath the calm, the passion flies.
With every breath, the truth unfolds,
A love that's more than silence holds.

No longer bound by fear or shame,
Our hearts declare in love's own name.
From shadows drawn, the truth assessed,
A secret love is now confessed.

Beyond the Vow

In whispers soft, with hearts aligned,
We pledged a love both deep and kind.
Beyond the vow, through journeys grand,
Together we shall always stand.

With every dawn and setting sun,
Our bond remains, forever one.
Through trials faced and tears we weep,
This promise we shall always keep.

In laughter shared and silent nights,
Our love shines through, a guiding light.
Though winds may howl and tempests rage,
We'll weather storms, page after page.

For love that's true, so pure, so bright,
No shadow dims our endless light.
Beyond the vow, our souls entwined,
In you, my love, my heart I find.

Just Because

A rose for you, just because,
Of all you are, and all you does.
In every smile and gentle touch,
You're why my heart loves so much.

No special day, no grand event,
Just moments shared, and time well spent.
In every laugh and tender glance,
You've given love another chance.

For love's not bound by date or time,
But in the quiet, it's sublime.
Simple acts, in little ways,
Create our brightest, happiest days.

Just because, for love is true,
In every word, professed anew.
For in your eyes, I see my dreams,
And feel the love that softly gleams.

Unpredicted Presents

In moments when you least expect,
Life offers gifts we can't neglect.
Unpredicted presents, filled with grace,
Surprise our hearts, a warm embrace.

A sudden laugh, a tear of joy,
A newfound hobby to enjoy.
A friend who calls, out of the blue,
A love that's tender and so true.

For life holds secrets, hidden well,
In every sound, in every smell.
Each simple gift, a cherished thing,
A song of love within us sings.

So let us cherish every day,
For unpredicted gifts do stay.
With open hearts, let's welcome all,
For in their light, we stand tall.

Heartfelt Impulses

A touch, a smile, a swift embrace,
Heartfelt impulses we can't erase.
In every deed, a love so pure,
Moments fleeting, yet so sure.

A sudden kiss, a whispered word,
A quiet song, softly heard.
In every hug and gentle squeeze,
Love's tender warmth, a calming breeze.

For impulses guide, where heart does lead,
In every action, every deed.
They're signs of love, of care, of trust,
In them we find, the bond is just.

So let us cherish these small signs,
For in them, endless love aligns.
Heartfelt impulses, pure and true,
Remind us of the me and you.

Promises in the Shadows

In the silence of twilight
Where shadows softly creep
Lies a world of whispered vows
And secrets that we keep

Beneath the silver moon
In the hush of night,
A thousand promises bloom
Away from the light

Footsteps echo in the dark
Where dreams and fears blend
In the shadows, questions spark
As promises ascend

The night holds its breath
As whispers intertwine
Between life and death
A spectral, unseen line

When dawn finally breaks
And shadows lose their hold
The night, with promises it takes
Leaves stories yet untold

The Gift of Unspoken Love

In the quiet glance we share
A garden of dreams blooms
Silent words weave in the air
Painting pastel rooms

Your touch, a gentle whisper
On my heart's silent page
Each gesture a fleeting tremor
Of love that never ages

No voice to break the spell
No sound to mar the grace
In silence, we both dwell
In love’s warm, tender space

Eyes meet in knowing gleam
A symphony unsaid
In the stillness, we redeem
The words better unread

This love, a secret kept
Safe in the heart’s deep cove
Where no noise has ever crept
The gift of unspoken love

Acts of Unexpected Benevolence

A kind smile, a warm embrace
From strangers passing by
An unexpected, gentle grace
Bestowed without a sigh

In moments unforeseen
With kindness softly sown
A light where once was lean
A kindness brightly shown

The world, a tapestry
Of lives that intertwine
Kindness flows so silently
In acts so small, divine

A helping hand, a whispered cheer
As hearts in kindness bloom
Through acts that dry a tear
And light the darkest room

Benevolence in silence
With love and grace to mend
In unexpected kindness
Find peace around the bend

Hearts That Couldn't Restrain

In the wild beat of the heart
Where passion fiercely sways
Lies a fire that can't depart
Through calm or stormy days

Eyes that meet and then ignite
A flame that can't be tamed
In shadows of the quiet night
Hearts are then unchained

Their whispers break the silence
Through words both sharp and sweet
In secret acts of defiance
Their longing comes complete

Torn between the worlds they know
And flames they can't contain
They revel in love's brilliant glow
And hearts that couldn't restrain

One look, one touch, one breath
Is all it takes to start
A tale that neither life nor death
Could ever tear apart

Unspoken Exchange

Eyes that meet in silent grace,
Words unspoken leave their trace.
Hearts connect without a sound,
In this quiet, truth is found.

Fingers brush in fleeting touch,
Promises that mean so much.
Silent smiles, the secrets shared,
In this stillness, love declared.

Moonlit nights and whispered dreams,
Nothing's ever as it seems.
Souls entwine in gentle dance,
In the silence, sweet romance.

Stars above, a silent choir,
In their glow, hearts conspire.
Bound by threads of unseen art,
In the quiet, we impart.

Soft as shadows, shadows cast,
Moments linger, never past.
Unspoken words that softly blend,
In this silence, we transcend.

Hidden Tokens

In the folds of life's grand tale,
Lie secrets, whispers frail.
Hidden tokens, silent keys,
Unlocking dreams from wistful seas.

In the woods where shadows play,
Mysteries of the bygone day.
Ancient whispers in the trees,
Tokens left by gentle breeze.

In the lines of weathered face,
Stories time could not erase.
Hidden tokens, crafted fine,
Legacies in silent sign.

Underneath the star's soft light,
Secrets shimmer, silent night.
Tokens in the sand we find,
Echoes of the heart and mind.

Between the words on every page,
Lies the wisdom of an age.
Hidden tokens, small and bright,
Guiding us through dark and light.

Love’s Quiet Offerings

Morning light on dewdrop's sheen,
Whispers of what love could mean.
Gentle touch and soft caress,
Silent vows that hearts confess.

In the stillness of the night,
Promises seem ever bright.
In love’s quiet, offerings pure,
Tender moments that endure.

A single rose, a whispered prayer,
Tokens of the love we share.
In each glance, a world’s refrain,
Heartfelt whispers, sweet and plain.

In the hush of twilight’s kiss,
Love’s true form we often miss.
Yet it’s there in every breath,
Quiet songs of life and death.

Hands that hold without a sound,
Hearts that speak when lips are bound.
In love’s quiet, offerings sweet,
Find the place where soulmates meet.

Beneath the Ribbon

Beneath the ribbon, secrets hide,
Whispers of a life inside.
Tales of joy and sorrows deep,
Hidden where the shadows sleep.

Layers hold the worlds unseen,
Underneath the ribbon's sheen.
Delicate as morning dew,
Dreams are waiting there for you.

Gifts adorned with loving care,
Promises and hopes laid bare.
Beneath the ribbon, mysteries bloom,
Inside every silent room.

In the folds and gentle curves,
Lies the strength that love preserves.
Beneath the ribbon, hearts align,
Tales untold through hands entwine.

Wrapped in silk, a tender kiss,
Secrets held in pure abyss.
Beneath the ribbon, softly tied,
Lies the truth we cannot hide.

Beyond Vows and Promises

In twilight hours, dreams unfold,
Where whispered secrets softly told,
Eclipse the sun with tender grace,
In quiet moments, hearts embrace.

Beyond the vows, our spirits fly,
Infinite visions in the sky,
Promises fade as stars appear,
Eternal love, forever near.

Each stolen glance, a silent song,
The world unnoticed, spins along,
In realms where only we exist,
Our souls collide in twilight mist.

For every word, an untold tale,
In whispered winds, our voices sail,
Beyond the realm of time and space,
Our love discovered, every place.

Beyond the vows and spoken verse,
Lies beauty few can comprehend,
In silent vows, our truths immerse,
Together, always, till the end.

More Than Words Allowed

In quiet scenes where shadows play,
Our hearts commune without delay,
More than words can thus convey,
In sacred silence, love's display.

A single glance, a tender touch,
Conveys the meanings words can't clutch,
Moments silent, deeply loud,
More than words are here endowed.

Whispers born on nature's breeze,
Echo truths as spirits ease,
Silent vows in hearts enshrouded,
More than words, our love allowed.

Eclipsing phrases spoken loud,
Expressions silent, yet so proud,
In the realm where feelings shroud,
More than words, emotions crowd.

Understanding found profound,
In spaces where no sound is found,
Hearts entwined in silent vow,
More than words can e'er allow.

Joy Found in Forbidden Acts

In shadows cast by hidden glades,
Where sunlight dances, secrets fade,
A joy, clandestine, boldly stirs,
In echoes where the heart incurs.

Forbidden paths our footsteps trace,
In whispered realms, a safe embrace,
No boundary found within our sight,
As love ignites the night in spite.

Sneaking kisses, playful teases,
In places hidden, time releases,
Joy discovered, not allowed,
In acts forbidden, passion proud.

Silent vows in moonlit spaces,
Heartfelt notes in hidden places,
In shadows where our secrets spent,
A joy unfound in daylight's rent.

A love so strong where rules defied,
In secret moments, we abide,
Joy in acts the world disclaims,
In forbidden, love proclaims.

Breaking the Agreed Silence

In moments held by silent screams,
Our hearts contend with hidden dreams,
Breaking silence, words now loud,
In whispered truths we are unbowed.

Agreed silence falls apart,
As echoes pulse from heart to heart,
Words unspoken, guarded tight,
Now released in dawning light.

A look, a touch, no longer mute,
Feelings chime in crystal flute,
Breaking silence, gates unlock,
All our hidden thoughts to stock.

Silent realms where secrets kept,
No longer hold where we have wept,
Breaking silence, love is claimed,
In tender whispers, souls reclaimed.

The silence, fragile, split in two,
Replaced by love so pure and true,
Breaking all the walls once firm,
In our hearts, no silence spurned.

Quiet Inclusions

Beneath the shade of whispering trees,
The gentle hum of life's soft plea,
Moments stitched in the quilt of time,
Unseen, yet they gently chime.

The hush of dawn in morning mist,
A silent breath, a fleeting gist,
Nature's secrets, quiet and meek,
Inclusions rare, for hearts to seek.

Shadows dance on twilight's call,
Soft echoes in the starlit sprawl,
Hidden gems in the day's long hours,
Quietly burst into blooming flowers.

In the silence, treasures lie,
Every glance, a deepened sigh,
Whispers carried on the breeze,
Quiet inclusions, finding ease.

Daylight fades to night's embrace,
Gentle shifts in time and space,
Moments marked, both large and small,
Quiet inclusions, treasured all.

Gifts of the Soul

In the heart's most tender place,
Where true love leaves its trace,
Gifts of the soul, unseen, unheard,
In the silence, gently stirred.

A whisper shared, an unseen smile,
Moments that linger, all the while,
Tokens of kindness, from mind to mind,
Timeless treasures, soul-defined.

A touch that warms in deepest cold,
Stories of the heart, richly told,
Boundless love, a soft embrace,
In every soul, it finds a space.

Feelings deep, like roots unseen,
In times of joy, and times between,
Gifts of spirit, strong and true,
Soul's light that shines through you.

Silent vows, in shadows cast,
Love’s whispers, made to last,
Gifts of the soul, forever pure,
In each heart, love’s signature.

Silent Rebellion

In the quiet, a storm brews near,
A whispered plan, devoid of fear,
Silent acts, in shadows veiled,
Rebellion born, where light had failed.

Softest steps on hidden trails,
In the silence, courage prevails,
Voices rise without a sound,
In the heart, rebellion found.

A glance that speaks a thousand words,
Silent wings of unseen birds,
Against the tide, quiet strides,
In the calm, the storm resides.

Breath withheld, yet loud as thunder,
Invisible chains, quietly sunder,
Bold gestures in the still of night,
Silent rebellion, out of sight.

In the hush, a world transfixed,
Voiceless calls of change betwixt,
Silent rebellion, strong and bright,
In the dark, there lies the light.

Tokens of Unseen Love

In whispers soft, in gentle gaze,
Love's tokens form in secret ways,
Silence speaks where words may fail,
Unseen love in whispers pale.

A fleeting touch, a glance so slight,
In the shadows of night's cloak of light,
Tender moments, softly framed,
Love unseen, but hearts proclaimed.

In the quiet of dawn’s embrace,
In every look upon your face,
Tokens of love, unseen, but known,
In silence, affection shown.

Soft serenades in breathless air,
Silent vows that lovers share,
Unseen threads of love’s deep loom,
In every touch, in every room.

The echoes of a love so pure,
In every heart, forever sure,
Tokens of love, invisible yet,
In every moment, no regret.

Surprising Tenderness

In the shadows soft and near,
A gentle touch, a whispered cheer,
Surprising tenderness unfolds,
In the quiet, warmth beholds.

A kindness hidden in the night,
A beacon in the dimmest light,
Unexpected, sweetly shown,
A love that's silently grown.

With each gesture, hearts align,
In the silence, they entwine,
Tender moments, unforeseen,
In the hush, true love is seen.

From the dark, compassion springs,
In the silence, softly sings,
Surprising hearts with gentle art,
Tenderness that melts the heart.

In the stillness, souls connect,
With a grace they don't expect,
Surprising tenderness revealed,
In love's quiet, softly healed.

Secrets in Wrapping

Beneath the crinkled, colored wrap,
Lies a secret, held with a clasp,
In the folds, a quiet charm,
Gifting hearts, a gentle balm.

In the layers, whispers hide,
Truths that time and space confide,
Secrets wrapped in love's pure thread,
Tender words left softly said.

Each layer peeled reveals a clue,
A hint of something deep and true,
Wrapped in moments, fleeting fast,
Memories from the distant past.

In the ribbons, lies and dreams,
Hidden lightly in the seams,
Secrets wrapped in simple grace,
Moments that no time can erase.

Untwine the ribbons, gentle hands,
Unfold the whispers, understand,
Secrets held in wrapping tight,
Revealed in love's forgiving light.

Unveiled Emotions

Behind the masks we choose to wear,
Lies a heart that's deeply fair,
Emotions hidden, seldom seen,
In the soul's quiet serene.

Unveiled with a gentle glance,
In the light, our hearts can dance,
Emotions freed from shadowed walls,
Answering the love that calls.

A tear that falls, a smile that blooms,
In the silence, love resumes,
Emotions raw, unveiled and true,
In the gaze shared just by two.

Behind each laugh, a whisper's plight,
Emotions stir, take silent flight,
Unveiled in moments pure and clear,
Hearts revealed, forever near.

Let the shield now fade away,
Embrace the night, welcome day,
Unveiled emotions, freely flow,
In love's light, let feelings show.

Unexpected Treasure

In the mundane, a glint of gold,
A story brightens, yet untold,
An unexpected treasure found,
In common ground, hearts unbound.

Among the ordinary days,
A special spark, a loving gaze,
Unexpected beauty gleams,
In the simple, tender dreams.

A whispered word, a fleeting smile,
Touches hearts and stays a while,
Unexpected treasure is there,
In the moments, love laid bare.

In the quiet, mundane times,
Love's sweet rhythm subtly rhymes,
Unexpected joy and pleasure,
In life's small, hidden treasure.

Embrace the unexpected gift,
In the simple, spirits lift,
Treasure found in places slight,
A love that's kept in tender light.

Touched by Unplanned Joy

In gardens wild, the daisies grow,
Sunlight caught in morning dew,
Unplanned wonder, soft and slow,
Gifts found in moments new.

Laughter spills from loamy soil,
Children chasing dreams untamed,
Life itself becomes the spoil,
Of the joy no hand has claimed.

An echo in the woods so deep,
Whispered tales of bliss unearned,
Here we dance, awake from sleep,
Touched by joy, our hearts affirmed.

Streams of gold in twilight's sheen,
Through the haze of day’s descent,
Captured in a realm serene,
Unplanned joy, a time well spent.

Under stars, our wishes weave,
Embraced by all the night can give,
Serendipity, we believe,
In this moment, we truly live.

Beyond the Silent Rules

In shadows where the rules don't reach,
Whispers of a secret free,
Lives are lived beyond the breach,
Silent steps of liberty.

Eyes meet eyes and words unspoken,
Speak a language soft and clear,
Trust in silence, bonds unbroken,
Hearts aligned with no frontier.

No command or voice rehearsed,
Guides the path of hidden ways,
In the quiet, we immerse,
Living out our mute displays.

Beneath the surface lies a world,
Crafted by the nameless, bold,
Where the silent truth unfurled,
Is more priceless than pure gold.

Infinite the paths we tread,
Not by order, byte or file,
But by dreams and visions led,
Dancing past the silent isle.

Acts of Quiet Defiance

In the held-back breaths, a storm,
Silent acts that shift the tide,
Steps of courage, hearts so warm,
In their quiet, strength implies.

Unseen rebellions, daily strife,
Moments seized without a claim,
Living true to one's own life,
Even when the world's the same.

Beneath the surface, currents flow,
Power in a gentle gaze,
Lighting up the depths we know,
Finding freedom in the haze.

Tiny sparks in endless night,
Acts of quiet, fierce resolve,
In the darkness, worlds ignite,
And around them, truths revolve.

Whispered secrets shape our lives,
Sacred tendrils, quiet force,
Through the silence, hope survives,
And defiance finds its course.

Favors Beyond Promises

Kindness in the subtle ways,
Gifts unbound by words or ties,
Silent favors, humble praise,
Echoes in the soft goodbyes.

Gentle hands when life is hard,
Lending strength without a vow,
Acts of grace no strings have marred,
Daily love in the here and now.

Beyond the promises, we live,
Tiny sparks of light and care,
Compassion that our souls forgive,
Binding hearts with threads so rare.

In moments unassumed and brief,
Given freely, no demand,
Healing others in our grief,
Lifting spirits on the sand.

Favor found in smallest deeds,
Far beyond what words convey,
Nurtured by unspoken creeds,
In the light of day-to-day.

Unexpected Declarations

In midnight's hush, confessions rise,
Unfurling truths beneath cold skies.
Unseen, unheard, words take flight,
Whispered soft in shadowed night.

Eyes meet eyes, a silent plea,
Hearts unbound, yet wild and free.
Secrets churned in hidden streams,
Unveiling souls with quiet dreams.

Tentative beginnings, tender breath,
Life's vibrant pulse, defying death,
Courage blooms in darkened rooms,
Mapping love's uncharted tombs.

Lips align, a tremor felt,
Silent pacts in darkness knelt,
Promises in heartbeats blend,
Echoes of declarations penned.

Shadows fade, dawn's light ascends,
Echoed vows in future trends,
Steps once hesitant, now strong,
Songs of love, the morning's song.

Love’s Whimsy

Whims of heart, sweet and errant,
Capturing moments, transient, apparent.
Laughter echoes, joy’s embrace,
Dancing through time, a tender grace.

Moonlit paths, serendipity’s reign,
A fleeting kiss amidst the rain.
Stolen glances, a game of chance,
Hearts entwined in fleeting dance.

Petals twirl in twilight's hue,
Dreams of love, forever new.
Candles flicker, shadows play,
Whispers trace the light of day.

Grains of sand, through fingers slip,
Memories held in fingertips.
Ephemeral bonds, yet deeply tied,
Waves of love, an endless tide.

Whimsical, wild, untamed yet true,
Love’s dance, an endless debut.
Moments fleeting, yet ever near,
In love’s whimsy, no space for fear.

Surreptitious Delights

Cloaked in shadows, secret found,
Hidden joys, without a sound.
Eyes that spark in candle's glow,
Unknown paths where lovers go.

Quiet hands in quiet night,
Fingers trace the edges light.
Softest whisper, touch so sweet,
Worlds collide where shadows meet.

Echoes in the midnight air,
Caresses light, beyond compare.
Hearts in secret, bold desires,
Warmed by love’s surreptitious fires.

Footsteps on a moonlit lane,
Unseen paths that leave no stain.
In the dark, a furtive glance,
Unspoken words in silenced dance.

Moments vanish with the dawn,
Yet the echoes linger on.
In the heart, a sweet delight,
Hidden love that burns so bright.

Unuttered Affection

Silent vows beneath the stars,
Unspoken love that's never far.
Glimmering eyes in twilight’s glow,
Secrecy the heart bestows.

Unuttered words, a tender phase,
Lovers lost in mutual gaze.
Breathless whispers fill the air,
Souls entwined with hidden care.

Smiles that speak without a voice,
Hearts compelled by silent choice.
Canvas stretched in hues of light,
Painting love in silent night.

Gestures soft, a hand’s caress,
Words within, yet unexpressed.
Feeling deep, as oceans wide,
In silence, hearts are deified.

Morning breaks, the secret kept,
Promises in quiet stepped.
Love unvoiced, yet understood,
Eternal, silent, pure and good.

Gifts Beyond the Unspoken Rule

In shadows cast by silent law,
Where whispers reign, unseen but raw,
Beneath the veil of night we find,
Gifts of heart, unasked, unlined.

Through secret paths where few may tread,
Uncharted dreams, bright threads do spread,
Beyond the rule, unloosed, unfurled,
A hidden grace, a quiet world.

No proclamation, loud or brash,
Just kinship's touch, without a clash,
In twilight's glow, we come to see,
The gifts we give to hearts set free.

In day's decline, where shadows grow,
Beyond the words, the gestures show,
In secret smiles, the world's made whole,
With gifts that don't a price extol.

For in the dark, a truth revealed,
That love, in stealth, has always healed,
These gifts beyond what rules decree,
Bind us, in secret harmony.

Undisclosed Acts of Kindness

In moments hushed, in silences,
Where kindness thrives without pretense,
Unseen hands weave tender tales,
Of hearts that break and love prevails.

Through gentle acts, the world is stitched,
With threads of care in seams unhitched,
Undisclosed, these whispers blend,
To lift us up and help us mend.

Where shadows cloak the brightest deeds,
In soft retreats and fitting needs,
A helping hand, no banners flown,
Speaks louder than the loudest tone.

In silent grace, a heart abides,
In quiet depths where love resides,
These acts, unseen, yet deeply sown,
In kindness, all our spirits grown.

For in the warmth of softest touch,
Lies the power to heal so much,
These undisclosed, yet guiding lights,
Illuminate our darkest nights.

Quiet Gestures of Love

In gentle glances, hearts embrace,
Without a word, they find their place,
In silence, love's soft touch is found,
A bond that's felt, yet makes no sound.

Through quiet gestures, lives entwine,
A simple note, a sign, a line,
These unvoiced vows, no need for show,
In stillness, tender feelings grow.

Unspoken ties, they bind us fast,
Beneath the noise, they forever last,
A loving touch, a knowing smile,
Keeps us close across the miles.

In moments hushed, affection blooms,
In shadowed nooks and sunlight rooms,
Quiet gestures paint our skies,
With hues of love that never dies.

For in the calm, love's voice is clear,
Unshouted, yet it draws us near,
These quiet gestures, simply true,
Are timeless threads that weave us through.

Twilight of Forbidden Gifting

In twilight’s hush, where secrets dance,
A world beyond first glance,
Forbidden gifts in shadows glow,
With tales untold, in softest flow.

Where night unfolds its velvet shroud,
The heart’s desires are avowed,
In whispers, gifts slide into view,
In secrecy, they find their due.

The twilight bears our hidden dreams,
Where nothing’s quite as it seems,
A gift that’s passed in shadow’s throw,
Holds the warmth the sun won’t show.

Yet in this realm, our spirits soar,
Unbridled by the day’s decor,
Forbidden gifts, in twilight’s gleam,
Are fragments of a deeper dream.

In time’s expanse, where shadows play,
These hidden gifts alone will stay,
In twilight’s grace, our hearts entwined,
In secret love, forever blind.

Acts of Quiet Generosity

In subtle ways, with silent grace,
We change the world, a softer place.
Through acts unseen and often mild,
Generosity, undefiled.

A helping hand, a gentle deed,
Fulfilling every silent need.
In moments small, a gift proceeds,
Kindness planted, love succeeds.

With quiet strength, we lift and share,
Creating hope from true, deep care.
In whispers, gestures, softly made,
Generous hearts, light's serenade.

Invisible yet shining bright,
Acts of love through day and night.
In every heart, a spark ignites,
Generosity's simple rites.

In shadows where we often tread,
Acts of kindness widespread.
Through silent realms, our spirits fly,
In generous acts, we reach the sky.

The Hidden Touch of Affection

In unseen threads, affection weaves,
A tapestry that never leaves.
Hidden touch, a gentle sway,
Binding hearts in soft array.

In quietude, love's touch is found,
A silent echo, all around.
In every glance and subtle tone,
Affection's hidden, yet brightly shown.

The brush of hands, a fleeting glance,
In love's embrace, a silent dance.
Whispered words, a sweet caress,
Affection's touch, pure tenderness.

Through moments still, hearts intertwine,
In hidden ways, our love does shine.
With every breath, a soft caress,
Affection's touch, our souls confess.

In secret places, love does dwell,
In every touch, its story tell.
Hidden paths where hearts connect,
The touch of love, pure and perfect.

Milton Keynes UK
Ingram Content Group UK Ltd.
UKHW022359220724
445930UK00003B/40

9 789916 763100